SIR FRANCIS DRAKE
His Daring Deeds

ROY GERRARD

FARRAR STRAUS GIROUX   NEW YORK

When Francis Drake was only ten,
   he went to sea with grown-up men,
And flabbergasted all the crew
   by quickly learning what to do.

He fathomed ways of wind and tide,
in storms he just brushed fear aside.
He learned to steer and read a map —
lionhearted little chap!

One day while sailing — dearie me,
the ship's cat toppled in the sea.
Drake dived right in and grabbed the cat —
he saved its life, just fancy that!

Young Francis grew up strong and straight,
a small but sturdy heavyweight,
And on his twenty-seventh trip
was made the captain of a ship.

He joined a fleet which planned to go
exploring parts of Mexico,
But when they reached those distant lands,
they found the place in Spanish hands.

The Spaniards bowed and smiled and waved,
  they seemed extremely well behaved.
The English thought it would be best
  to anchor there and have a rest.

At dawn next day the Spaniards crept
to rob the sailors as they slept.
But Drake awoke, "To arms!" he roared,
and drove the Spaniards overboard.

Then cannonballs flew overhead —
some ships sank; the English fled.
Drake muttered, as he put to sea,
"They haven't heard the last of me."

They struggled back to England's shore,
　　but Francis soon set sail once more.
The Spanish ships he came across
　　quickly learned that Drake was boss.

He sank their ships and took their gold,
　　but treated prisoners well, we're told;
For though revenge was on his mind,
　　he found it hard to be unkind.

Drake chased the Spaniards near and far,
then went ashore in Panama.
He caught some Spanish chaps whose mules
bore bulging sacks of gold and jewels.

High on a ridge, he climbed a tree
    to scan the wide Pacific sea.
"By Jove," said Drake, "I'd like to try
    and sail that ocean, by and by."

Back home, he studied maps and charts
   that told of strange, exotic parts,
Then took his leave, with sails unfurled,
   to circumnavigate the world.

To South America they went,
   and forged right round that continent.
They had a rough and stormy ride
   while sailing the Atlantic side.

Two ships they burnt, to cook their meat
    (and dry their clothes and toast their feet).
They felt much better after that,
    and likewise their bedraggled cat.

Up surged a storm, the wild winds blew,
a ship was sunk with all its crew.
Another turned and headed home,
yet Francis battled on alone.

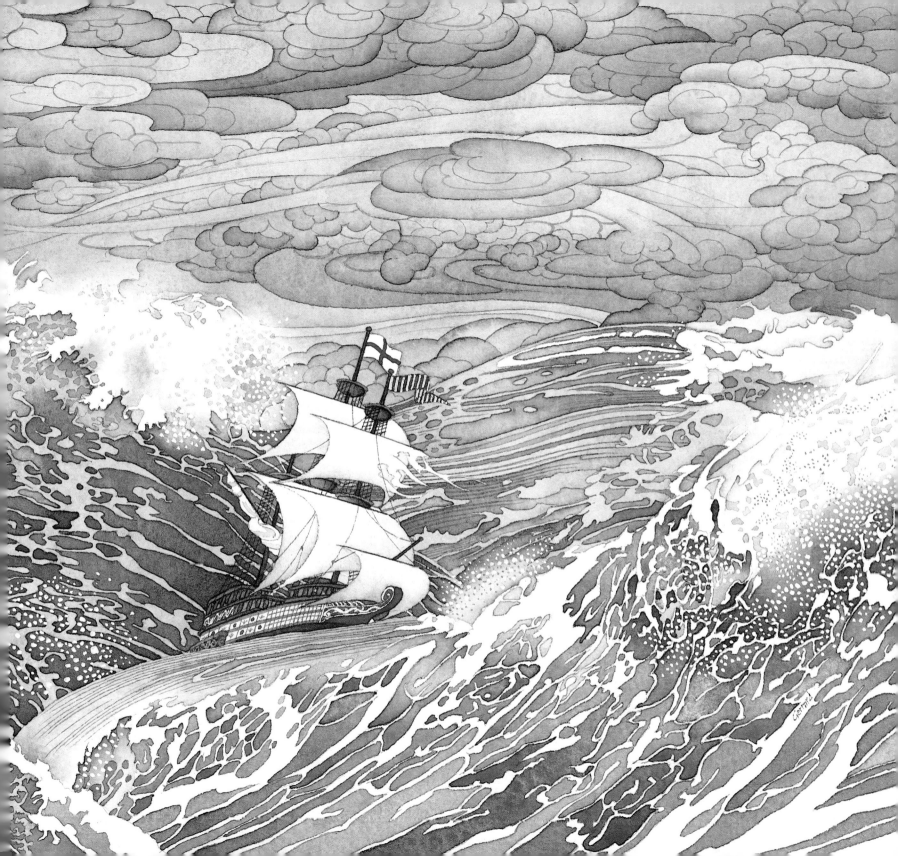

They went ashore to have a nap,
but local tribes had set a trap.
And Drake, exhausted by the fight,
decided it was time for flight.

Next, woe is me — an awful shock,
their ship stuck fast upon a rock.
Attempts to free it seemed in vain,
then, slowly, it slid off again.

In distant seas and tropic climes
   the gallant crew found better times,
But, tiring of their global tour,
   returned to England, safe once more.

When Francis entered Plymouth Sound,
   a mighty crowd soon gathered round.
And Queen Elizabeth came, too,
   to welcome Francis and his crew.

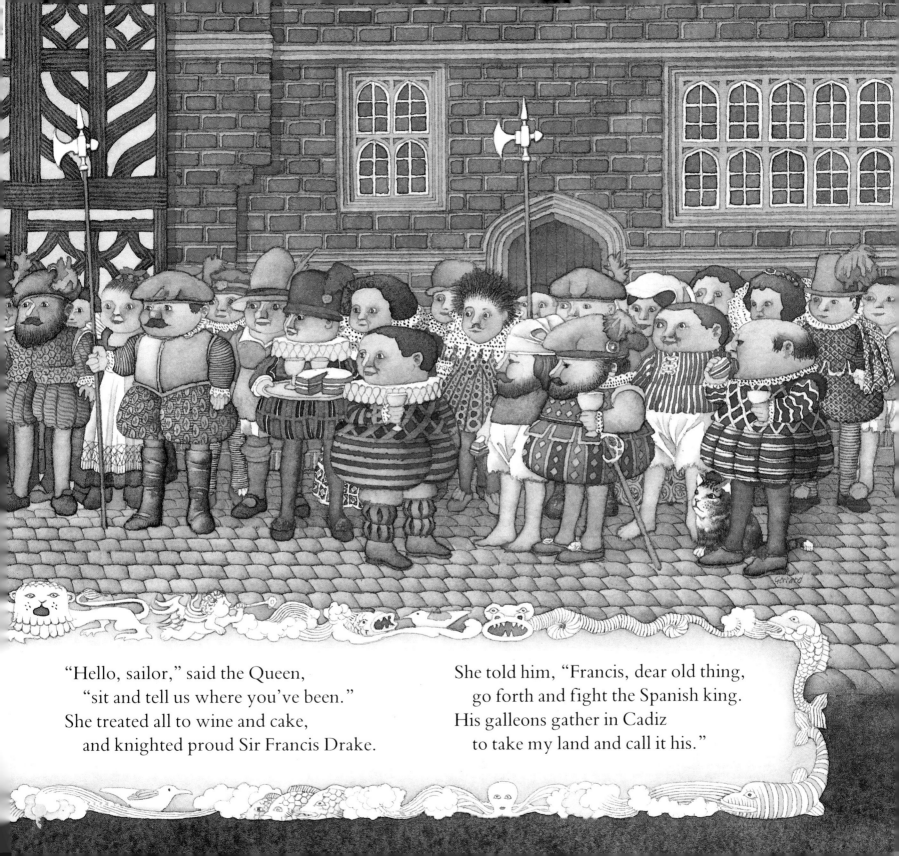

"Hello, sailor," said the Queen,
  "sit and tell us where you've been."
She treated all to wine and cake,
  and knighted proud Sir Francis Drake.

She told him, "Francis, dear old thing,
  go forth and fight the Spanish king.
His galleons gather in Cadiz
  to take my land and call it his."

Francis, always keen for action,
  rubbed his hands in satisfaction.
He hailed the fleet and steered for Spain
  to face those Spaniards once again.

Now, in Cadiz Sir Francis Drake
  spied his foes just half awake.
He sank their ships, ransacked the town,
  and burnt their mighty castle down.

Back at home, his kinsmen cheered
  to hear he'd singed King Philip's beard.
The Queen of England, much impressed,
  said, "Well done, Drake. Now take a rest."

Drake took a break and went away
  to have a well-earned holiday.
Relaxing now, with carefree thoughts,
  he filled his days with games and sports.

But as he played at bowls one day
  a frantic message came to say,
"A brand-new Spanish fleet's been seen —
  come quickly, Francis," signed, "The Queen."

Drake finished off his game, of course,
  then gathered up his fighting force.
And sailing forth, soon came to grips
  with all the waiting Spanish ships.

King Philip's craft were tall and slow,
the English vessels fast and low;
They darted out and in again
among the clumsy ships of Spain.

They fired their guns with such effect
that many Spanish ships were wrecked.
The discombobulated foe
decided it was time to go.

SIC PARVIS MAGNA

Sir Francis swished his sword with glee
to see the grand Armada flee.
He sent a message to his fleet,
"Well done, brave lads — revenge is sweet."

The English sailors, pleased and proud,
sped home to face a joyful crowd.
Their queen, Elizabeth the Great,
laid on a feast to celebrate.

She said, "You steadfast sailors all,
   who bravely answered England's call,
Have put the Spanish fleet to shame
   and earned yourselves undying fame.

"At least four hundred years from now
   your tale will still be told, I vow.
My bold Sir Francis, valiant crew,
   England will remember you."